DUDLEY SCHOOLS LIBRARY
AND INFORMATION S

KU-393-708

Schools Library and Information Services

S00000672452

My
Body

Paul Humphrey

Photography by Chris Fairclough

W
FRANKLIN WATTS
LONDON • SYDNEY

First published in 2005 by
Franklin Watts
96 Leonard Street
London EC2A 4XD

Franklin Watts Australia
Level 17/207 Kent Street
Sydney NSW 2000

© 2005 Franklin Watts

DUDLEY PUBLIC LIBRARIES

L 48001

672452 SCH

J 612

ISBN 0 7496 6173 9 (hbk)
ISBN 0 7496 6185 2 (pbk)

Dewey classification number 612

All rights reserved. No part of this publication may be
reproduced, stored in a retrieval system, or transmitted
in any form or by any means, electronic, mechanical,
photocopying, recording or otherwise, without the prior
written permission of the copyright owner.

A CIP catalogue record for this book is available
from the British Library.

Planning and production by Discovery Books Limited
Editor: Rachel Tisdale
Designer: Ian Winton
Photography: Chris Fairclough
Series advisors: Diana Bentley MA and Dee Reid MA,
Fellows of Oxford Brookes University

The author, packager and publisher would like to thank the following
people for their participation in this book: Ottilie and Auriel Austin-Baker;
Toby Frampton; Samiya Latif and Arrandeep Bola.

Printed in China

Contents

This is my body.

eye

ear

nose

mouth

teeth

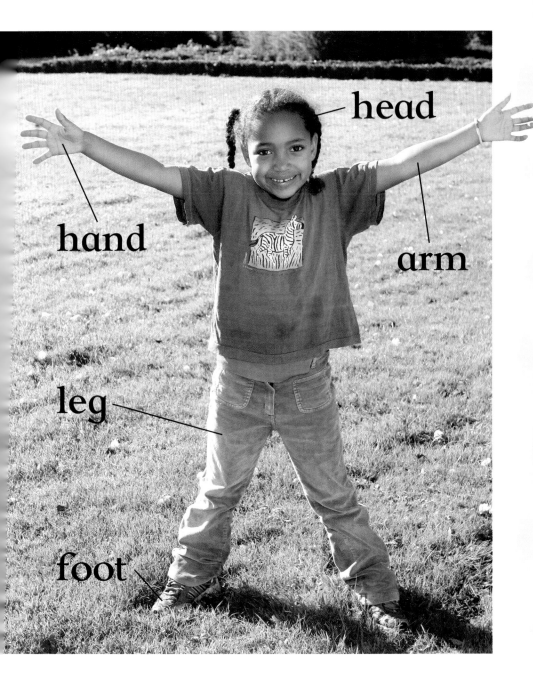

head

hand

arm

leg

foot

I use my
hands to beat
the drum.

I use my
feet to kick
the ball.

I can smell
the flower
with my
nose.

I can see the book
with my eyes.

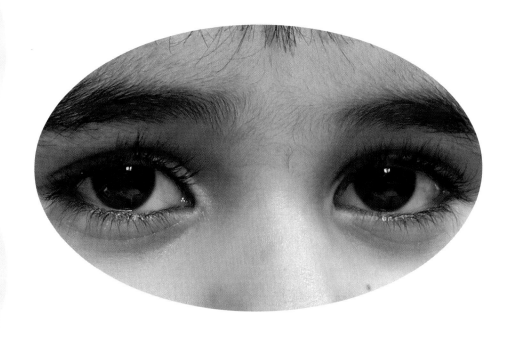

We talk with our mouths.

We listen with
our ears.

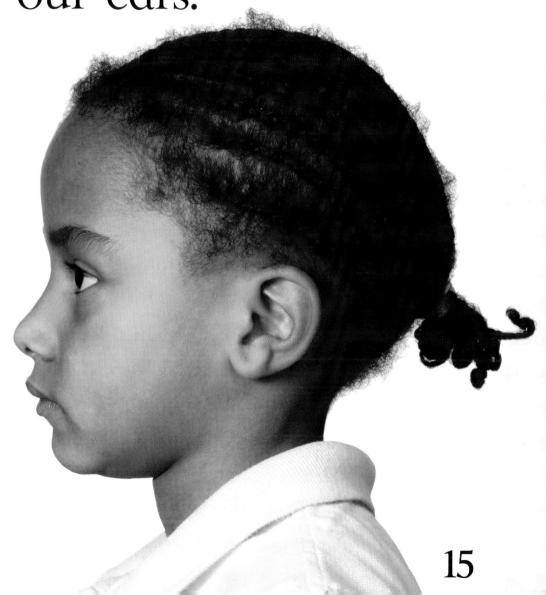

Our arms
are good for
climbing.

17

Our legs are
good for jumping
and running.

My teeth
can bite
the apple.

Our bodies are great!

23

Word bank

Look back for these words and pictures.

Arms

Ears

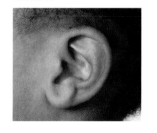

Eyes

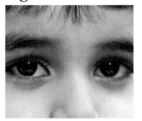

Feet

Hands

Legs

Mouths

Nose

Teeth